Illustrated Phrasal Verbs

Jill **looks after** her grandmother so well.

Can you believe that Anne is turning 18 next week? She **grew up** so fast!

Mrs. Jones **brought up** her children to be kind, considerate adults!

Sheila certainly **took after** her mother. They look just alike!

Illustrated Phrasal Verbs

Preface

Phrasal verbs are verbs that consist of two or three parts (a verb and an adverb, a verb and a preposition, or a verb, an adverb, and a preposition) which together have a completely different meaning than the meaning of the verb.

Phrasal verbs are very important in English and quite difficult for students to learn. Some of the most common ones are dealt with in this book.

The book aims to build up students' knowledge of phrasal verbs through full colour illustrations, which are accompanied by graded exercises.

In the first page of each unit, students are presented with the new phrasal verbs, their definitions and an example in context. Then, in the following two-page spread, students have to match the verbs with the illustrations and complete the sentences that describe them.

In the subsequent pages, there are exercises that aim to help students revise the verbs that they have seen in the presentation pages of the unit.

There are two Revision Exercises Tests each covering 5 Units.

The book can be used in the classroom, or for self-study purposes. The exercises can be given as homework and then discussed in class.

Published by
GLOBAL ELT LTD
60 Pankhurst Avenue, Brighton,
East Sussex, BN2 9YN, UNITED KINGDOM

www.globalelt.co.uk

Copyright © GLOBAL ELT LTD
The right of Andrew Betsis and Lawrence Mamas to be identified as the authors of this work has been asserted in accordance with the Copyright, Designs and Patent Act 1988.

All rights reserved.
No part of this publication may be reproduced, stored in a retrieval system,
or transmitted in any form or by any means, electronic, mechanical, photocopying,
recording or otherwise, without the prior permission in writing of the Publisher.
Any person who does any unauthorised act in relation to this publication maybe
 liable to criminal prosecution and civil claims for damages.

- ILLUSTRATED PHRASAL VERBS - LEVEL B2 - TEACHER'S BOOK   ISBN: 978-1-904663-04-1
- ILLUSTRATED PHRASAL VERBS - LEVEL B2 - STUDENT'S BOOK   ISBN: 978-1-904663-05-8

British Library Cataloguing-in-Publication Data
A catalogue record of this book is available from the British Library.

Contents

UNIT 1	Page 5
UNIT 2	Page 11
UNIT 3	Page 17
UNIT 4	Page 23
UNIT 5	Page 29
REVIEW UNIT: UNITS 1-5	Page 35
UNIT 6	Page 41
UNIT 7	Page 47
UNIT 8	Page 53
UNIT 9	Page 59
UNIT 10	Page 65
REVIEW UNIT: UNITS 6-10	Page 72
PHRASAL VERBS INDEX	Page 76
IRREGULAR VERBS INDEX	Page 78

Illustrated Phrasal Verbs

The structure of each Unit:

The phrasal verbs are presented with their definitions at the beginning of the unit.

Full colour illustrations show what each phrasal verb means, accompanied by Activity A (matching/gap-filling).

A variety of Exercises help students master the use of the most frequent phrasal verbs.

Fun activities to revise the phrasal verbs are provided at the end of each unit.

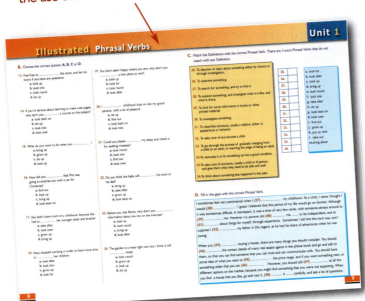

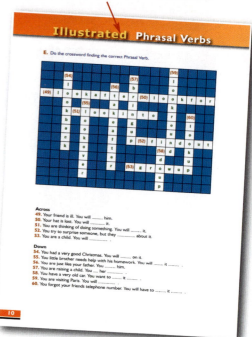

UNIT 1

PHRASAL VERBS

find out	look over	look for	look round
look up	look into	take after	bring up
grow up	do up	look after	look back on

find out - discover something you did not know, or learn about it either by chance or through investigation
e.g. *I only found out about the exam a few days ago.*

look over - examine something
e.g. *What did you think of the essay that you looked over for Mike?*

look for - search for something, and try to find it
e.g. *If you need help finding what you're looking for, just let me know.*

look (a)round - explore something, and try to understand what it is like
e.g. *I looked (a)round for months before I decided which car to buy.*

look up - look for information in reference books
e.g. *Did you find conflicting opinions when you looked the information up?*

look into - investigate something
e.g. *Is Lucy looking into adopting a puppy?*

take after - look like someone (a relative), resemble someone in appearance or behaviour
e.g. *Jeremy so takes after his mother!*

bring up - take care of children and educate them
e.g. *He was brought up to value honesty highly.*

grow up - to gradually change from a child to an adult
e.g. *Jocelyn grew up more quickly than her twin brother did.*

do up - renovate something (eg. property) or make it look almost as good as new
e.g. *Mr. Brown does up old houses and then sells them for a living.*

look after - take care of someone (ill) and offer them what they need to be safe and well
e.g. *You could tell that the children were not well looked after.*

look back on - think about something that happened in the past
e.g. *I spent a lot of time last winter looking back on the previous summer.*

Illustrated Phrasal Verbs

A. Fill in the gaps in the sentences below with the correct Phrasal Verb from unit 1.

1. If you're not sure when the plane is leaving, why don't you ask someone and *find out*... ?

4. Before leaving, Tom *looked over* his new bicycle carefully.

2. It can be a challenge to *look for*... your glasses if you cannot see without them.

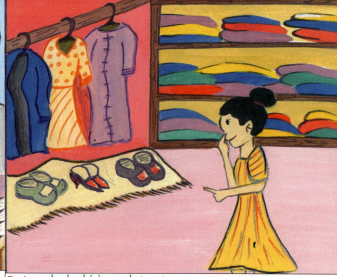

5. Anna *looked (a)round* the shop quickly and then decided on a pair of light blue shoes.

3. John *looked up*... the number of a plumber in the telephone book because the kitchen tap would not stop dripping.

6. I think you should call the police. They will *look into* why the baby was abandoned.

Unit 1

7. Amy certainly ..takes after.. her mother, doesn't she! They look just alike!

10. Mrs. Smith ..brought up... her children to be kind, considerate people.

8. Can you believe that Maria is turning 18 next week? It seems like she ..grew up.. so fast!

11. They wanted to find an old cottage in the country that they could buy cheaply, and then ..do up... .

9. Jessica ..looks after..... her grandmother so well; she always has time to help her with shopping, or just take her out.

12. My grandfather always likes to ..look back on.. when my mother and uncle were my age.

7

Illustrated Phrasal Verbs

B. Choose the correct answer **A**, **B**, **C** or **D**.

13. Feel free to .... the store, and let me know if you have any questions.
    a. look up
    b. look into
    c. look (a)round
    d. do up

14. If you're serious about learning to make web pages, why don't you .... a course on the subject?
    a. look back on
    b. do up
    c. look into
    d. look over

15. What do you want to do when you .... ?
    a. bring up
    b. grow up
    c. do up
    d. look up

16. How did you .... that Phil was going to surprise you with a car for Christmas?
    a. find out
    b. look up
    c. bring up
    d. look back on

17. She didn't have much of a childhood, because she had to .... her younger sister and brother.
    a. take after
    b. look over
    c. grow up
    d. bring up

18. Stacy stopped working in order to have more time to .... her children.
    a. look after
    b. look into
    c. grow up
    d. look for

19. You don't seem happy where you are; why don't you .... a new place to rent?
    a. look up
    b. look for
    c. look (a)round
    d. look after

20. I .... childhood trips to my grandparents with a lot of pleasure.
    a. do up
    b. find out
    c. look back on
    d. look into

21. Could you please .... my essay and check it for spelling mistakes?
    a. look (a)round
    b. look into
    c. find out
    d. look over

22. Do you think the baby will .... his mum or his dad?
    a. bring up
    b. take after
    c. grow up
    d. look back on

23. Before you visit Rome, why don't you .... information about the city on the Internet?
    a. look up
    b. look (a)round
    c. bring up
    d. look after

24. The garden is a mess right now but I think we will .... it .... nicely.
    a. look ... (a)round
    b. grow ... up
    c. look ... up
    d. do ... up

Unit 1

C. Match the Definitions with the correct Phrasal Verb. There are 3 extra Phrasal Verbs that do not match with any Definition.

25. To discover or learn about something either by chance or through investigation.
26. To examine something.
27. To search for something, and try to find it.
28. To explore something, and investigate what it is like, and what is there.
29. To look for some information in books or other printed material.
30. To investigate something.
31. To resemble someone, usually a relative, either in appearance or behaviour.
32. To take care of and educate a child.
33. To go through the process of gradually changing from a child to an adult, or reaching the stage of being an adult.
34. To renovate or make it look almost as good as new.
35. To take care of someone, usually a child or ill person, and give them what they need to be safe and well.
36. To think about something that happened in the past.

25.	k
26.	j
27.	a
28.	e
29.	c
30.	f
31.	g
32.	d
33.	l
34.	h
35.	b
36.	i

a. look for
b. look after
c. look up
d. bring up
e. look (a)round
f. look into
g. take after
h. do up
i. look back on
j. look over
k. find out
l. grow up
m. put up with
n. take out
o. bring about

D. Fill in the gaps with the correct Phrasal Verb.

A look back at my childhood!

I sometimes feel very sentimental when I (37) **look back on** my childhood. As a child, I never thought I would (38) **grow up**; I guess I believed that this period of my life would go on forever. Although it was sometimes difficult, in retrospect, it was a time of very few cares, with someone always around to (39) **look after** me. However, my parents did (40) **bring** me **up** to be independent, and to (41) **find out** about things for myself, through experience. Sometimes I did this the hard way, and I suppose I (42) **take after** my father in this regard, as he had his share of adventures when he was young.

House-hunting tips!

When you (43) **look into** buying a house, there are many things you should consider. You should (44) **look up** the contact details of many real estate agents in the phone book and go and talk to them, so that you can find someone that you can trust and can communicate with. You should have some idea of what you want to (45) **look for** - the price range, and if you want something new, or something older, which you can later (46) **do up**. However, you should still (47) **look round** at all the different options on the market, because you might find something that you were not expecting. When you find a house that you like, go and visit it, (48) **look** it **over** carefully, and ask a lot of questions.

9

Illustrated Phrasal Verbs

E. Do the crossword finding the correct Phrasal Verb from unit 1.

										(59)			
		(54)					(57)			l			
		l			(56)		b			o			
(49)	l	o	o	k	a	f	t	e	r	(50)	l	o	o	k	f	o	r
		o		(55)		a		i			k			
		k	(51)	l	o	o	k	i	n	t	o		(60)	
		b		o		e		g			r		l	
		a		o		a		u			o		o	
		c		k		f		p	(52)	f	i	n	d	o	u	t
		k		o		t			(58)	d		k	
				v		e				d		u	
				e		r	(53)	g	r	o	w	u	p
				r						u			
										p			

Across

49. Your friend is ill. You must .... him.
50. Your hat is lost. You will .... it.
51. You are thinking of doing something. You will .... it.
52. You try to surprise someone, but they .... about it.
53. You are a child. You will ....

Down

54. You had a very good Christmas. Later in life, you will .... on it.
55. Your little brother needs help with his homework. You will .... it ....
56. You are just like your father. You .... him.
57. You raise a child. You .... her ....
58. You have a very old car. You want to .... it ....
59. You are visiting Paris. You will ....
60. You forgot your friend's telephone number. You will have to .... it ....

UNIT 2

PHRASAL VERBS

put through	speak up	cut off	hold on
get through (1)	stand for	break down (1)	break up (1)
break off	make up (1)	make up for	fall out

put through - You put a caller through on the telephone when you connect them with the person they want to speak to.
e.g. *I was on hold for twenty minutes before I was put through to the right department so that I could make my complaint.*

speak up - You speak up when you talk more loudly than before.
e.g. *Could you speak up a bit? We can't hear you at the back of the room.*

cut off - Someone or something is cut off when it is disconnected or interrupted.
e.g. *His telephone line was cut off because he didn't pay his bill.*

hold on - You ask someone to hold on when you want them to wait.
e.g. *Hold on a minute; let me turn off the car's engine before you open the door!*

get through (1) - You get through to someone when you succeed in contacting them by telephone.
e.g. *Oh, I'm so glad I finally got through to you; I need to tell you I won't be at the meeting tomorrow.*

stand for - An abbreviation stands for a word or set of words that it represents or refers to.
e.g. *W.W.F stands for the World Wildlife Fund.*

break down (1) - When machinery breaks down, it stops working.
e.g. *I only carry a mobile phone in case my car breaks down on some deserted highway.*

break up (1)- People break up when their relationship or partnership comes to an end.
e.g. *Fans can feel very sad when their favourite bands break up.*

break off - You break something off when you end, discontinue or interrupt it.
e.g. *Talks between the two countries will break off if they don't reach an agreement soon.*

make up - People who have quarrelled, make up when they settle their differences and become friends again.
e.g. *At the end of the movie, the lovers kissed and made up.*

make up for - You make up for something wrong that you have done when you do something nice as an apology.
e.g. *I'm so sorry I was late; let me treat you to lunch to make up for it.*

fall out - People fall out when they quarrel.
e.g. *It is a shame when families fall out over trivial things.*

Illustrated Phrasal Verbs

A. Fill in the gaps in the sentences below with the correct Phrasal Verb from unit 2.

1. Hello, can you *put* me *through* to the office of Mr. Brown please?

4. You have to *speak up* when you are talking to grandma, because she is very hard of hearing.

2. The line got *cut off* while Tommy and his grandmother were talking.

5. The letters W.W.W. *stand for* the World Wide Web.

3. Can you *hold on* for a moment? We've just received a very important fax on the other line.

6. After trying all day to phone him, George finally *got through* to his friend.

Unit 2

7. I'm afraid I can't offer you an espresso because my espresso machine ..broke down... this morning!

10. The children ...broke off.. their collaboration when they couldn't agree on a topic for the report.

8. Their marriage ...broke up... after only a year and three months.

11. Anna's boyfriend ...made up for.. being late by bringing her a big bouquet of flowers.

9. John and Tina have a turbulent relationship; they are always fighting and then ...making up... again.

12. The friends planned a lovely picnic, but unfortunately they ...fell out... and then neither felt like eating it.

13

Illustrated Phrasal Verbs

B. Choose the correct answer **A**, **B**, **C** or **D**.

13. Do you know what W.H.O. .... ?
    a. makes out
    b. breaks down
    c. stands for
    d. makes up for

14. My sister and I .... regularly but we always forgive each other after a couple of days.
    a. make up
    b. fall out
    c. break off
    d. cut off

15. Jill's husband forgot their anniversary, but then bought her a necklace to .... his absentmindedness.
    a. make up
    b. break up
    c. make up for
    d. stand for

16. If the line gets .... just hang up the phone; I'll call you back.
    a. put through
    b. cut off
    c. broken up
    d. fallen out

17. Some people would rather .... than have a long-distance relationship.
    a. hold on
    b. make up
    c. break up
    d. fall out

18. You need to .... and say what you believe or else you are going to get frustrated.
    a. get through
    b. speak up
    c. break off
    d. break down

19. I wouldn't .... negotiations quite yet; give them some time to think.
    a. stand for
    b. cut off
    c. stand for
    d. break off

20. Dr. Jones is in the laboratory this afternoon; let me .... you .... to the lab.
    a. cut ... off
    b. put ... through
    c. get ... through
    d. break ... off

21. Helen, I'm not sure you two should .... ; he's definitely no good for you.
    a. break up
    b. fall out
    c. break off
    d. make up

22. It will take all day to .... to the computer helpline; it will be quicker to solve the problem myself.
    a. get through
    b. put through
    c. hold on
    d. cut off

23. .... a moment please, let me check my diary.
    a. Stand for
    b. Make up
    c. Hold on
    d. Make up for

24. It is inevitable that your computer will .... a few days before the deadline.
    a. fall out
    b. break up
    c. break down
    d. hold on

14

Unit 2

C. Match the Definitions with the correct Phrasal Verb. There are 3 extra Phrasal Verbs that do not match with any Definition.

25. To connect someone with the person they want to speak to
26. To talk more loudly than you did before
27. To disconnect or interrupt something
28. To wait for someone or something
29. To succeed at reaching someone by telephone
30. To represent a word or groups of words using an abbreviation
31. When machinery stops working
32. When a relationship or partnership comes to an end
33. To end, disrupt or interrupt something
34. To settle your differences and become friends again
35. To apologize for doing something wrong by doing something nice
36. To quarrel

25.	g
26.	c
27.	n
28.	m
29.	a
30.	b
31.	i
32.	j
33.	o
34.	f
35.	h
36.	e

a. get through
b. stand for
c. speak up
d. do up
e. fall out
f. make up
g. put through
h. make up for
i. break down
j. break up
k. look back
l. bring up
m. hold on
n. cut off
o. break off

D. Fill in the gaps with the correct Phrasal Verb.

Failing to get through!

When my brother was studying in Ireland, it was very difficult to (37) *get through* to him on the telephone. First of all we had to call his university, then ask to be (38) *put through* to the residence hall where he was staying, and there were about twelve students sharing this phone line, so it was usually busy. If someone answered they would inevitably say (39) *hold on* while I go and try to find Mark, and we would wait and wait! Also the line wasn't good; it was full of static and we really had to (40) *speak up*. Often, when the weather was bad, the line would (41) *cut off* completely.

Back in the day!

There was one time in my childhood when my parents very seriously (42) *fell out*. It was over a silly thing, really. My mother was driving somewhere, I can't remember where, and the car (43) *broke down*. She tried to call my Dad and couldn't get through to him. I think she left the car in the street and took a taxi home. When my Dad got home he made some comment like "What? Don't you remember what RAC (44) *stands for*?" We had paid Rescue Auto Care money to come and help us if we had car trouble, but Mum forgot all about them. She was so angry that she (45) *broke off* all communication with Dad. I really thought that they were going to (46) *break up*. But Dad surprised her with a holiday to (47) *make up for* being so rude, and I guess they (48) *made up* then because everything was back to normal when they returned.

15

Illustrated Phrasal Verbs

E. Do the crossword finding the correct Phrasal Verb from unit 2.

Across
49. You've done something wrong and feel guilty. You want to .... it.
50. You fought with your partner. You miss him and want to ....
51. EU is an abbreviation. It must .... the European Union.
52. Your sister insults you every time you see her. You decide to .... relations with her.
53. You need help dialing a number. The operator can .... you ....
54. I can't hear you! Please ....
55. You two can't agree on anything. You always ....
56. I didn't pay my bill, so the electricity was ....

Down
57. My car is making funny noises. It will probably .... soon.
58. Your marriage doesn't seem to work. It will soon ....
59. You called your bank with a question. They asked you to .... while they find your information.
60. His phone line was busy all day. You couldn't ....

16

UNIT 3

PHRASAL VERBS

drop in	run into	come into	run in
come across	get round (1)	break out in	break down (2)
go down	pass out	get over	come round/come to

drop in - You drop in when you pay a short visit, often without warning.
e.g. *I was running errands in the neighbourhood this morning, so I thought I would drop in and see how you are.*

run into - You run into someone when you meet them unexpectedly.
e.g. *Michelle didn't go to the party because she didn't want to run into her ex-boyfriend.*

come into - You come into money when you inherit it.
e.g. *Since he came into his fortune, he has been spending his time working for several charities.*

run in - You run something in, such as an engine, when you use it carefully until it is ready for normal use.
e.g. *You shouldn't drive too fast in your new car because you need to run in the engine.*

come across - You come across something when you discover or encounter it without looking for or expecting it.
e.g. *He came across a wallet in the park so he turned it in to the police.*

get (a)round (1) - You get round a problem when you solve or avoid it.
e.g. *He got round the problem of not having a car by moving nearer to his job.*

break out in - You break out in something, such as a rash or sweat, when there is a sudden spread of it on your body.
e.g. *She won't walk up the stairs because she is afraid she will break out in a sweat.*

break down (2) - You break down when you lose control emotionally.
e.g. *When he heard that his grandfather had died he broke down and cried.*

go down - Something goes down when it reduces, falls or gets lower.
e.g. *If your fever doesn't go down by tomorrow, you should call a doctor.*

pass out - Someone passes out when they become unconscious for a short time.
e.g. *She was taken to hospital after she passed out and hit her head when she fell.*

come (a)round/come to - someone who is unconscious comes round or comes to when they regain consciousness.
e.g. *I was feeling a bit dizzy; then, the next thing I knew, I came round on the ground surrounded by a crowd of people.*

get over - You get over something such as an illness, shock or disappointment when you recover from it
e.g. *I hope you get over the flu quickly!*

Illustrated Phrasal Verbs

A. Fill in the gaps in the sentences below with the correct Phrasal Verb from unit 3.

1. I was thinking of you today and thought I would just ...drop in.... for a coffee!

4. Mr. Jones ...got round... the problem of moving his fridge by tipping it onto a trolley and rolling it.

2. The two friends ...ran into.... each other on the street after not meeting for over ten years..

5. Jose ...ran in.. the engine of the new motorbike with great care.

3. The boy ...came across..... fifty pounds lying in the road.

6. When her uncle died, Beth ...came into. a large amount of money.

Unit 3

7. When Eve had the chicken pox she **broke out in** spots.

10. When I saw the man **pass out**, I was very glad I'd had first aid training and knew what to do!

8. When Mich heard that his family was going to move, he **broke down** and started crying uncontrollably.

11. She **came round** to find herself in a quiet room with a hot cup of tea on a low table near her.

9. It's a good sign that the swelling has **gone down**; you'll be back to normal in a few weeks.

12. Luckily Gemma **got over** her illness quickly and left the hospital after only one day.

Illustrated Phrasal Verbs

B. Choose the correct answer **A**, **B**, **C** or **D**.

13. If she swims in a chlorinated pool, Mary Ann will .... a rash.
    a. get over
    b. come into
    c. break out in
    d. go down

14. If you over heat and don't drink enough water you could ....
    a. pass out
    b. go down
    c. get round
    d. get over

15. Do you mind if your friends .... unannounced?
    a. get round
    b. run in
    c. come round
    d. drop in

16. Someone threw water on the unconscious man and he .... , coughing and sputtering.
    a. came round
    b. passed out
    c. came across
    d. got over

17. There is no way to .... having to pay taxes.
    a. get round
    b. get over
    c. come into
    d. come across

18. After I sprained my wrist, it took several days for the swelling to ....
    a. go down
    b. break out in
    c. get over
    d. run in

19. How long did it take you to .... the flu?
    a. come into
    b. break out in
    c. come across
    d. get over

20. I .... Larry almost every time I go out to eat at this restaurant.
    a. come round
    b. get over
    c. run into
    d. get round

21. Bri .... a fair bit of money when she turned twenty one.
    a. broke out in
    b. got over
    c. passed out
    d. came into

22. Be sure to .... your new tyres; don't push them too hard right away.
    a. come into
    b. get over
    c. get round
    d. run in

23. Did you .... any jewellery in the ladies room? I've lost a bracelet..
    a. come into
    b. come round
    c. drop in
    d. come across

24. Her co-workers teased her until she finally .... and started screaming at everyone.
    a. came round
    b. broke down
    c. passed out
    d. went down

Unit 3

C. Match the Definitions with the correct Phrasal Verb. There are 3 extra Phrasal Verbs that do not match with any Definition.

25. To pay a short unexpected visit
26. To meet someone unexpectedly
27. To inherit money
28. To carefully use something new
29. To discover something you were not looking for or expecting
30. To solve or avoid a problem
31. To appear suddenly on the body
32. To lose control emotionally
33. When something falls or is reduced
34. To become unconscious for a short while
35. To regain consciousness
36. To recover from something

25.	g
26.	f
27.	n
28.	a
29.	l
30.	b
31.	d
32.	k
33.	o
34.	i
35.	e
36.	h

a. run in
b. get round
c. fall out
d. break out in
e. come round/come to
f. run into
g. drop in
h. get over
i. pass out
j. put through
k. break down
l. come across
m. find out
n. come into
o. go down

D. Fill in the gaps with the correct Phrasal Verb.

An itchy red rash!

Last weekend Julie (37) **broke out** in a itchy red rash. It looked bad, but luckily she (38) **got over** it quickly and the rash had (39) **gone down** on its own by Monday. We (40) **got round** making a trip to the doctor by looking up rashes on the internet, and decided she had an allergy. However, on Monday at school she (41) **passed out** and although she (42) **came to**, right away, she was rushed to hospital by ambulance. We found out that she had the measles and we had to keep her at home, isolated for a week. No friends were allowed to (43) **drop in** because she was very contagious!

Billy's flashy car!

Guess who I (44) **ran into** yesterday! Billy! I was walking down 31st Street, and he drove past in a very expensive looking car, and waved at me. I almost didn't recognize him. He stopped, and we chatted for a bit. His big news was that he had (45) **come into** quite a bit of money - more than most people (46) **come across** in their lifetime! I don't think he is managing it wisely though. He said he (47) **broke down** when his parents died, and then decided he should buy the car of his dreams even though it was totally impractical. He was out (48) **running** it **in** when our paths crossed.

21

Illustrated Phrasal Verbs

E. Do the crossword finding the correct Phrasal Verb from unit 3.

Across
49. You find a new computer in a box on the road. When you ………. it, you are surprised!
50. A flu can make you feel like you are dying, but you will ………… it.
51. You haven't seen your friend in ages. You were in the neighbourhood so you decided to ………… .
52. You don't give up easily. You will …………… the problem somehow.
53. You go to the same supermarket as Anna. You …………… her all the time there.

Down
54. You are allergic to shampoo. You ……………. a rash each time you use it.
55. If you feel dizzy, sit down. You could ……………. and fall.
56. Your grandfather became unconscious for a moment while driving. Luckily, he managed to ………. before there was an accident.
57. You feel very sad. You ……………. and cry in public.
58. You've had your wisdom teeth removed and your mouth is swollen. The swelling will …………… in about a week.
59. When her aunt Mary dies, she will ………… a lot of money.
60. We decided to …………. our brand-new car.

UNIT 4

PHRASAL VERBS

work out	point out	make out (1)	think over
come up with	make up (2)	hold up (1)	see off
drop off (1)	take off (1)	pick up	set off

work out - You work out a problem when you solve it by thinking about it carefully.
e.g. *I've worked out that we will save money if we double glaze the windows.*

point out - You point something out to someone when you indicate it in some way.
e.g. *It is not polite to point out when someone has gained weight.*

make out (1) - You make something out when you see or hear it, often with difficulty.
e.g. *I can't quite make out who that is waving at me from across the square.*

think over - You think something over when you consider it carefully in order to come to a decision.
e.g. *When he proposed to her she was surprised and said she would have to think it over.*

come up with - You come up with an idea when you think of it.
e.g. *I need to come up with some ways to save money.*

make up (2) - You make something up when you invent it, sometimes with the purpose of deception.
e.g. *When he was a child he made up the most amazing imaginary games.*

hold up (1) - You hold something up if you stop or delay it.
e.g. *Wearing steel-toed boots can hold you up when you try to go through airport security.*

see off - You see someone off when you say goodbye to them as they leave.
e.g. *She felt sad because there was no one to see her off when she was leaving.*

drop off (1) - You drop someone or something off when you take them someplace and then leave them there, often in a vehicle.
e.g. *Will you drop this package off at the post office this morning?*

take off (1) - An airplane or a bird takes off when it rises up from the ground and begins to fly.
e.g. *The birds all took off and flew away when they saw the cat.*

pick up - You pick someone up when you stop to give them a lift in your vehicle.
e.g. *We need to pick up Sara at her house on the way to the beach.*

set off - You set off when you begin a journey.
e.g. *When are you planning to set off on your travels?*

Illustrated Phrasal Verbs

A. Fill in the gaps in the sentences below with the correct Phrasal Verb from unit 4.

1. Lena didn't understand her maths assignment; however hard she tried she couldn't ...**work out**... the answer.

4. Bill ...**pointed**... the airplane ...**out**... to his little sister.

2. I can just barely ...**make out**... that that red spot in the distance is a boat.

5. David ...**thought over**... how to solve the Rubik's Cube for hours, then, amazingly, actually solved it in two minutes!

3. The person who ...**came up with**... the idea for this bridge was a genius!

6. Roy ...**made up**... an excuse about why he was late.

Unit 4

7. The man ..held up.. the line when he tried to pay with a hundred pound note, because they didn't have change.

10. Most people won't stop to ..pick up.. hitch-hikers.

8. She went to the port to ..see.. her son ..off.. when he got a job on a cruise ship.

11. The weather was lovely as they ..set off.. on their backpacking trip.

9. The plane ..took off.. from the runway and lifted into the air.

12. She was lucky her husband could ..drop.. her ..off.. at the station because she had a lot of luggage.

Illustrated Phrasal Verbs

B. Choose the correct answer **A, B, C** or **D**.

13. Can you .... me .... on [in] the High Street on your way to work?
    a. point ... out
    b. see ... off
    c. drop ... off
    d. set ... off

14. I think that accident is going to .... traffic for miles!
    a. hold up
    b. pick up
    c. take off
    d. make up

15. Give me a call when the party is over and I'll come and .... you ....
    a. bring ... up
    b. pick ... up
    c. see ... off
    d. take ... off

16. I can't .... what that sign says; the letters are too small.
    a. point out
    b. set off
    c. see off
    d. make out

17. It's a good idea to have some food and something to read with you when you.................. on a train journey.
    a. think over
    b. set off
    c. take off
    d. work out

18. Will you come to the airport to .... me .... when I leave for university?
    a. take ... off
    b. see ... off
    c. pick ... up
    d. set ... off

19. You don't need to .... some reason why you can't make it; if you don't want to come, just say so!
    a. work out
    b. point out
    c. make up
    d. hold up

20. Miles thinks he's .... a plan to earn a million dollars.
    a. set off
    b. come up with
    c. made up
    d. made out

21. The airplane could not .... because of dense fog.
    a. set off
    b. hold up
    c. take off
    d. make up

22. I just can't .... what all these charges on my phone bill are for!
    a. work out
    b. point out
    c. make out
    d. think over

23. This car seems like what I'm looking for, but I will have to .... it ....
    a. point ... out
    b. make ... up
    c. work ... out
    d. think ... over

24. Excuse me, could you .... the way to the train station?
    a. point out
    b. see off
    c. make up
    d. come up with

Unit 4

C. Match the Definitions with the correct Phrasal Verb. There are 3 extra Phrasal Verbs that do not match with any Definition.

25. To solve a problem by thinking about it carefully
26. To indicate something, in some way, to someone
27. To see or hear something with difficulty
28. To consider something carefully before making a decision
29. To think of an idea
30. To invent something
31. To stop or delay something
32. To say goodbye to someone as he or she leaves on a journey
33. To take someone someplace and leave him or her there
34. To rise from the ground and begin to fly
35. To stop and give someone a lift
36. To begin a journey

25.	d
26.	e
27.	b
28.	m
29.	g
30.	a
31.	o
32.	f
33.	c
34.	k
35.	h
36.	n

a. make up
b. make out
c. drop off
d. work out
e. point out
f. see off
g. come up with
h. pick up
i. look back on
j. cut off
k. take off
l. break off
m. think over
n. set off
o. hold up

D. Fill in the gaps with the correct Phrasal Verb.

Backpacking in India!

Christopher has decided to go backpacking around India. He is planning to (37)...set off...... in September after he's graduated and earned some money. His parents suggested that he should (38)...think...it...over.. carefully and (39)...work out...... exactly how much it would cost each day. They (40)..pointed out. that it could be a problem if he ran out of money and couldn't afford to get home! His parents said they would (41)...drop...... him ..off.. at the airport, but his mother says she won't go in to (42)...see..him..off... . She says she will cry when the airplane (43) ..takes off..... .

Aliens are coming!

"Can you (44)...make out.. what that is in the sky? Look, drivers are stopping to look, and it's (45)......holding up.... traffic! Perhaps it's a flying saucer that is coming to (46)..pick...... us ..up.. !"
"You do like to (47) ....make up.... stories, don't you? I can't believe what you (48) ..come up with.... sometimes!

27

Illustrated Phrasal Verbs

E. Do the crossword finding the correct Phrasal Verb from unit 4.

					(56)								
				(49)	m	a	k	e	u	p			
			(55)		a				(58)			(60)	
			p		k		(57)		t			p	
	(50)	c	o	m	e	u	p	w	i	t	h	(59)	i
			i		o		o		i		d	c	
			n		u		r		n		r	l	k
			t		t		k		k	(51)	h	o	l	d	u	p
			o				o		o		p		p
		(54)	u				u		v		o		
(52)	s	e	t	o	f	f	(53)	t	a	k	e	o	f	f
	e								r			f	
	e												
	o												
	f												
	f												

Across

49. Your friend tells bizarre stories. You think he must .... them ....
50. Your teacher asks you a question. You have to .... an answer .
51. The roads are icy. This will .... traffic.
52. You are leaving tomorrow. You will .... early in the morning.
53. The plane is on the runway. It is ready to ....

Down

54. You are going away to college. Your parents will .... you ....
55. He forgot his sunglasses. You .... it .... to him .
56. You need glasses. It is hard to .... the blackboard from the back of the room.
57. This jacket is fifty percent off. You can easily .... how much is costs.
58. You don't know which job to take. You need to .... it ....
59. The train station is crowded and there's nowhere to park. You can just .... me ....
60. When the movie is over your dad will .... you ...... outside the cinema.

UNIT 5

PHRASAL VERBS

call off	put off (1)	be taken aback	be over
is off	give out	try on	wear out (1)
do up (2)	take off (2)	go with	put on

call off sth or call sth off (1) - An event or arrangement is called off when it is cancelled, or stopped [abandoned] after it has begun.
e.g. I'm afraid I have to call off my singing lesson this week because I have a sore throat.

put off (1) - You put something off when you delay doing it until a later date.
e.g. Why do you put off writing your essays until the night before they are due?

be taken aback - You are taken aback when you are surprised or confused by something.
e.g. I was taken aback when I found out that Judy had an identical twin.

be over - Something will be over when it has finished.
e.g. The movie will be over at 9pm if you want to meet for a meal afterwards.

sth is off (only in the present simple tense) - An event or arrangement is called off when it is cancelled.
e.g. Our economics lecture is off today because the professor is at a conference.

give out - You give things out when you give one to each of a number of people.
e.g. They will give out free books to everyone who comes to the lecture.

try on - You try on an article of clothing when you put it on to see if it fits.
e.g. I liked this skirt a lot until I tried it on, and then I changed my mind.

wear out (1) - You wear something out when you use it so much that it becomes weak or broken from use.
e.g. You will wear out you shoes quickly if you wear them every day.

do up (2) - You do something up when you fasten, button, zip, or tie it.
e.g. Adam needs to do up his shoelaces or else he may trip.

take off (2) - You take something off when you remove it from the body.
e.g. I always take off my shoes when I am at home.

go with - Something goes with something else when it matches or suits it.
e.g. I need to buy a belt to go with this dress.

put on - You put clothes on when you place them on your body, when you dress.
e.g. You have to put on a suit if you want to eat at that restaurant.

Illustrated Phrasal Verbs

A. Fill in the gaps in the sentences below with the correct Phrasal Verb from unit 5.

1. The volleyball game was ...called off... because of bad weather.

4. The teacher ...gave out... the exam papers at the beginning of the lesson.

2. Mary ...put off... cleaning her room for as long as she could.

5. Did you hear that tonight's concert ...is off...?

3. The storm ...was over... as suddenly as it had begun.

6. Timothy was ...taken aback... when he saw the man who was dressed up like a mummy.

Unit 5

7. Although the vest was old and ...worn out.... Jeremy could not bring himself to get rid of it.

10. Michael ...put on.... the green pullover before he went out in the cold.

8. Lisa has been ...trying on.... dresses for hours and she still can't decide which one to buy!

11. Do you really think that top ...goes with.... those plaid trousers?

9. If you don't ...do up.... the zipper of your jacket, it won't keep you warm.

12. She ...took off.... her coat and hat when she got to school.

Illustrated Phrasal Verbs

B. Choose the correct answer **A**, **B**, **C** or **D**.

13. You should unplug your computer until the lightning storm................. .
    a. is called off
    b. wears out
    c. gives out
    d. is over ✓

14. Andy always wears socks that .... his shirt.
    a. wear out
    b. do up
    c. put on
    d. go with ✓

15. Do you .... things like T-shirts or do you just buy them because you know they will fit?
    a. go with
    b. try on ✓
    c. do up
    d. wear out

16. If the performance .... I think we should get a refund.
    a. gives out
    b. is over
    c. is taken aback
    d. is off ✓

17. When a concert is ...., a new date is usually announced for those with tickets.
    a. put off
    b. called off ✓
    c. done up
    d. taken off

18. How do you have the patience to .... all those tiny buttons on your coat?
    a. wear out
    b. take off
    c. do up ✓
    d. try on

19. Wendy .... two pairs of socks to keep her new boots from giving her blisters.
    a. tried on
    b. put on ✓
    c. put off
    d. took off

20. George .... his new trousers because he did a lot of gardening while wearing them.
    a. wore out ✓
    b. tried on
    c. called off
    d. was taken aback

21. Margaret was .... when she saw a spider in the bathtub.
    a. done up
    b. worn out
    c. taken aback ✓
    d. taken off

22. It was impossible for Jose to .... getting his hair cut any longer; it was covering his eyes!
    a. try on
    b. put off ✓
    c. call off
    d. do up

23. Her sister always tells her that her outfits don't .... the shoes she likes to wear.
    a. take off
    b. try on
    c. go with ✓
    d. give out

24. We will .... a bottle of wine to the first ten customers that visit the new branch.
    a. put on
    b. put off
    c. give out ✓
    d. do up

Unit 5

C. Match the Definitions with the correct Phrasal Verb. There are 3 extra Phrasal Verbs that do not match with any Definition.

25. To cancel something that has already been scheduled
26. To delay doing something until a later date
27. To be surprised or confused by something
28. When something is finished
29. When an arrangement or event is cancelled
30. To give one of something to a number of people
31. To put on an article of clothing to see if it fits
32. To become weak or broken from use
33. To fasten, button or zip something
34. To remove an article of clothing from the body
35. To match or suit something else
36. To place clothing on the body

25.	k
26.	e
27.	f
28.	g
29.	i
30.	h
31.	n
32.	c
33.	l
34.	b
35.	o
36.	j

a. work out
b. take off
c. wear out
d. drop in
e. put off
f. be taken aback
g. be over
h. give out
i. is off
j. put on
k. call off
l. do up
m. make up
n. try on
o. go with

D. Fill in the gaps with the correct Phrasal Verb.

Shopping for boots

Last winter, I (37) **wore out** my favourite pair of boots. I was very sad, because I used to wear these boots almost every day. I had known for a while that the time was coming when I would have to replace them but I was (38) **putting** it **off** because I don't like shopping for footwear. But finally I couldn't delay any longer; I had to go shopping for boots. I was really (39) **taken aback** by what I saw! Does anybody really buy orange patent leather boots with three-inch heels? Or boots with 12 little buckles? I couldn't even find anything I wanted to (40) **try on**. I needed something that would (41) **go with** all of my clothes, that was easy to (42) **do up** in the morning and (43) **take off** again when I got home. And of course they would need to be comfortable from the moment I first (44) **put** them **on**.

It never rains but it pours!

Well, it looks like our trip (45) **is off**. In the end, the festival that we tried so hard to get tickets for has been (46) **called off** because the site is flooded from all the rain last week. The bad weather (47) **is over** now, apparently, but I guess there was damage that they can't repair easily. I certainly hope they will be (48) **giving out** refunds to all of us who got tickets!

Illustrated Phrasal Verbs

E. Do the crossword finding the correct Phrasal Verb from unit 5.

Across
49. Your blouse has 25 little buttons. It is difficult to ……… .
50. You need black trousers. They ………… almost everything.
51. Your friend keeps a pig as a pet in her apartment. You must ……… by that a bit, are you?
52. It looks like it will rain tomorrow. You should …………… the picnic.
53. You are promoting a concert. You …………… hundreds of flyers .
54. You don't like to vacuum. You always ……… it ……… .
55. If you wear your new jeans when you go hiking you might …….. them …….. .

Down
56. You hate lightning and thunder. You wish the storm would …………… .
57. You like that dress. You will ……… it …….. .
58. You are cold. You will ………… a pullover .
59. Your feet hurt. You want to ………… your shoes .
60. You need to get a refund. The concert ……… .

Review Units 1-5

Illustrated Phrasal Verbs

A. Match the first half of the sentence with the second half containing the correct Phrasal Verb.

1. When my brother left for college I went to the airport to
2. It is exciting when you are planning to
3. If you've sprained your ankle it may take a while for the swelling to
4. Mich, since you have the car today, can you
5. Since Jodie's father is ill I think we'd better
6. I wish this horrible party would
7. It's strange; even when inside, he never wants to
8. If you're going to be out in the sun all day, make sure to
9. See that purple speck in the distance? Can you
10. The line is not very good; I think we are going to
11. I don't feel safe in this house; I think we need to
12. Anna is not good at spelling; she needs someone to
13. He brought her a box of chocolates to
14. When you collapsed, I was afraid you were not going to
15. When you wear gloves, all the little buttons are difficult to
16. When some stores are trying to get business, they
17. My mother is the person who I most
18. Secondary school is not a time that I
19. There's someone at the door; could you please
20. By hanging up lots of posters I managed to

1.	n
2.	m
3.	c
4.	f
5.	l
6.	s
7.	o
8.	k
9.	q
10.	d
11.	t
12.	a
13.	i
14.	g
15.	e
16.	j
17.	r
18.	b
19.	p
20.	h

a. look over her essays.
b. look back on with pleasure.
c. go down.
d. be cut off.
e. do up.
f. drop the children off?
g. come to.
h. get round having to paint.
i. make up for being late.
j. give out discount coupons.
k. put on sunscreen.
l. call off the party.
m. set off on a journey.
n. see him off.
o. take off his sunglasses.
p. hold on a minute?
q. make out what it is?
r. take after.
s. be over soon!
t. look into moving.

Revision Test 1: Units 1-5

B. Write C or I in the box to the left (Correct or Incorrect) for each sentence using a Phrasal Verb.

21. The diplomats **broke off** communication.	21. C
22. They put us on a bus when the train **broke down**.	22. C
23. They are **bringing** their children **up** on holiday.	23. I
24. I need to **look up** how to spell that word; I can never remember.	24. C
25. Be sure to **do up** your house each time you go out.	25. I
26. Don't you dare **speak up** to me like that!	26. I
27. The best friends **fell out** over a silly misunderstanding.	27. C
28. I can't **get through** to Betty at home; I hope nothing's wrong!	28. C
29. I can't **stand for** ice cream, but I really love pizza.	29. I
30. Would you **pick up** someone you didn't know if their car had broken down?	30. C
31. Can you please **take** me **off** at the airport?	31. I
32. The street market is lovely, but it does **hold up** traffic.	32. C
33. I wanted to **get** the bridge **over** quickly because I'm afraid of heights.	33. I
34. He bruised his shoulder and **passed out** when he hit a chair as he was falling.	34. C
35. She **broke out in** a new dress for her birthday party.	35. I
36. Can you **run in** this book to the library? It's due today.	36. I
37. The telephone line has gone dead; we must have been **put through**!	37. I
38. Have you **found out** why you keep getting headaches?	38. C
39. At the end of the movie, the two estranged brothers **made up**.	39. C
40. That novel **is off**; it is not really worth your time or money.	40. I

Revision Test 1: Units 1-5

C. Fill in the gaps in the text with the correct tense of the Phrasal Verbs from the box below.

> - look after - break down - wear out - point out
> - be taken aback - break up - drop in - think over
> - put off - work out - make up - grow up
> - come up with - come into - run into - look round
> - come across - go with - try on - look for

Mysterious house

Something mysterious is going on at the house across the street. I can't quite **(41)** ...work out... exactly what it is that is so mysterious, but there is definitely something going on! I am always tempted to just **(42)** ...drop in.. one day, say hello, and **(43)** ..look round... , but I know that they would be **(44)** ...taken aback... and that makes me nervous so I **(45)** ...put..... it ...off.. . What I can say is that I can't, for the life of me, tell how many people are living there! I know a man lives there; I **(46)** ....run into..... him regularly around the neighbourhood, though we never speak. I thought he had a wife, but I don't see her at all anymore. Perhaps they **(47)** ..broke up. . Strangely though, it seems like he is **(48)** ..looking after.. several small children, and they all look alike! And on top of that, they have lived there for about five years, yet none of the children seem to **(49)** ..grow up.. ! I **(50)** ...pointed.. this ..out.. to another neighbour and he **(51)** ...came up with.... the idea that maybe they are ghosts! I think he may have been making fun of me, though, for some reason!

Buying a coat

I have just **(52)** ...come across a beautiful coat that I would like to buy. I **(53)** ....tried.... it ......on.. and it was wonderful. It **(54)** ....goes with......... the rest of my wardrobe perfectly. I need a coat too, because mine is **(55)** ....worn out... . I didn't buy it though because it was very expensive, and I have to **(56)** ...think...... it ..over. before spending that much money. To be realistic, unless I **(57)** .....come into... a small fortune I think I will have to **(58)** ..look for... something more affordable. Or, maybe, I will just give in and buy it. But then I will have to **(59)** ..make up... an excuse for why I can't pay the rent - not a good idea! I would probably **(60)** ..break down.. and cry if I were kicked out onto the street.

UNIT 6

PHRASAL VERBS

try out	give up (2)	catch on	give (oneself) up (1)
give up (3)	drop off	get round	go through
mistake for	be off (2)	take in	give in

give (oneself) up - You give yourself up when you surrender to someone in authority and become his or her prisoner.
e.g. After hiding out for several years, the fugitive gave himself up to the police.

catch on - Something catches on when it becomes popular.
e.g. I certainly hope that this style of high waisted trousers never catches on!

try out - You try something (activity, product etc.) out when you do it for the first time in order to find out if you like it or if it is useful.
e.g. If you've never windsurfed you should definitely try it out; it's one of my favorite sports!

drop off (2) - You drop off when you fall asleep.
e.g. I had to pull the car over and take a nap because I was starting to drop off at the wheel.

give up (2) - You give up, or give something up, when you stop trying to do it and admit defeat.
e.g. Tango is a difficult dance, so don't give up if you haven't got the hang of it in the first few lessons.

give up (3) - You give up something when you decide that you are not going to do it any longer.
e.g. I think my grandfather will give up driving because his eyesight is not very good.

get (a)round (2) - You get round, or get around, someone when you manage to persuade them to do something or let you do something.
e.g. Don't worry, my dad is easy to get round; he'll let me go on the trip in the end.

go off (1) - Something, usually food, goes off if it is not good to eat or drink any more because it is too old.
e.g. Does this milk smell like it's gone off to you?

go through - You go through something such as a room or container when you check its contents carefully.
e.g. I will have to go through my whole desk now because I can't find the paper anywhere.

give in - You give in when you admit that you've been defeated, or agree to stop opposing or resisting something and allow it.
e.g. Don't give in to the fashion industry and feel that you have to buy a whole new wardrobe every season.

take in - You are taken in by someone when you are fooled or deceived by them.
e.g. Don't let the dog take you in with her whining; she's not starving. I fed her an hour ago.

mistake for - You mistake someone or something for something or someone else when you wrongly think that they are the other.
e.g. A: "I have no idea who that was waving at me!"
B: "He must have mistaken you for someone else!"

Illustrated Phrasal Verbs

A. Fill in the gaps in the sentences below with the correct Phrasal Verb from unit 6.

1. When he saw that he was surrounded, the robber ...gave himself up... .

4. The trend of wearing baseball caps backward ...caught on... quickly among the children.

2. Have you ...tried out... the new exercise bike at the gym?

5. Oh, look! Dad has ...dropped off... in front of the television again.

3. When they found the horse, it had just about ...given up... from thirst.

6. Trevor is finally ...giving up... smoking!

42

Unit 6

Julie has the ability to ..get round... her mother, and get exactly what she wants!

10. The grapes looked lovely, but unfortunately they had ..were off.......... and tasted horrible!

The airport security ..went through.. every inch of Mr. Wallace's luggage.

11. Once Tommy saw that he could not win the fight and ..gave in....., the boys became good friends.

The security guard was ..taken in.. by the smuggler's friendly manner and did not search him.

12. Laura very nearly grabbed the snake because she had ..mistaken.. it ..for... a flower.

43

Illustrated Phrasal Verbs

B. Choose the correct answer **A, B, C** or **D**.

13. Why did you .... karate? I thought you enjoyed it!
    - **a. give up**
    - b. take in
    - c. give in
    - d. try out

14. I've always liked this kind of music but I never thought it would .... and become so popular.
    - **a. catch on**
    - b. give itself up
    - c. get round
    - d. take in

15. The politician said that he would never .... and meet the demands of terrorists.
    - a. give himself up
    - **b. give in**
    - c. go through
    - d. take in

16. Don't let the salesman .... you ......; it is not necessary to buy insurance for our houseplants!
    - a. give ... up
    - **b. take ... in**
    - c. mistake ... for
    - d. try ... out

17. People must .... him ...... his brother all the time because they look so alike.
    - a. get ... through
    - b. get ... round
    - c. take ... in
    - **d. mistake ... for**

18. Maria had to .... running the marathon when she twisted her ankle.
    - **a. give up**
    - b. give in
    - c. drop off
    - d. go off

19. MaryAnn hid her diary carefully so that her brother could not .... it and find out her secrets.
    - a. drop off
    - **b. go through**
    - c. get round
    - d. catch on

20. The driver involved in that hit-and-run accident should definitely .... to the police.
    - a. give in
    - b. give up
    - c. get round
    - **d. give himself up**

21. Michael is tired and will .... immediately if you put on a DVD to watch.
    - a. give up
    - b. give himself up
    - c. catch on
    - **d. drop off**

22. Do you think you can .... our teacher and convince her not to give us any homework tonight?
    - a. get through
    - **b. get round**
    - c. give in
    - d. take in

23. It is not very common for dried fruit to ....; it lasts a long time!
    - a. give up
    - b. drop off
    - **c. go off**
    - d. catch on

24. The new telephone company has an offer where you can .... the internet free for one month.
    - a. get round
    - **b. try out**
    - c. take in
    - d. give up

Unit 6

C. Match the Definitions with the correct Phrasal Verb. There are 3 extra Phrasal Verbs that do not match with any Definition.

25. To surrender to someone in authority
26. To become popular
27. To do something for the first time to see if you like it
28. To fall asleep
29. To stop trying to do something and admit defeat
30. To decide you will no longer do something
31. To persuade someone to do something or let you do something
32. To spoil and become rotten
33. To carefully check the contents of something
34. To admit that you've been defeated and stop resisting
35. To deceive someone
36. To think that something or someone is something or someone else

25.	j
26.	c
27.	m
28.	g
29.	f
30.	f
31.	d
32.	e
33.	l
34.	h
35.	n
36.	a

a. mistake for
b. look into
c. catch on
d. get round
e. go off
f. give up
g. drop off
h. give in
i. take on
j. give (oneself) up
k. fall out
l. go through
m. try out
n. take in
o. give away

D. Fill in the gaps with the correct Phrasal Verb.

Convincing Mum

Have you seen that new brand of cereal? I think it's called energy puffs. Anyway, I had really wanted to (37) **try** it **out** for a long time but my mother said it was rubbish. It's always difficult to (38) **get** her **round** to an idea and I had just about (39) **given up** trying when she brought a box home one day. Actually she had (40) **mistaken** it **for** something else and hadn't intended to buy it at all! I liked it a lot. You should definitely try it. I think it might (41) **catch on**. Mum however says that it tastes like it (42) **has gone off** and refuses to eat it.

On the run

After five months on the run after robbing the bank, with all that money to worry about, Timothy was ready to (43) **give** himself **up**. He had been (44) **taken in** by the dream of limitless wealth, but now he was ready to (45) **give up** that dream. He was just tired. Ever since he had had the money, every time he (46) **dropped off** he was immediately jolted awake by the thought that he might have left a packet of notes on a park bench with his fingerprints all over them and the police were coming. So Timothy went to the police. He showed them the money. Instantly, there were 10 guns pointing at him. "Don't shoot! I'm not dangerous, I (47) **give in**," he cried. The police took the money, (48) **went through** his pockets, and finally put the guns away and led him into the station to make a statement.

45

Illustrated Phrasal Verbs

E. Do the crossword finding the correct Phrasal Verb from unit 6.

Across
49. You robbed a bank and feel guilty. You will ....
50. You've lost your lip gloss. You will have to .... your purse.
51. If we don't finish that carton of milk, it will ....
52. You .... Beth ...... her sister often. They look alike.
53. Your parents wish that you lived near them. Eventually you .... and move .

Down
54. You have a lot of work today. You will .... it somehow.
55. You feel unhealthy. You will .... eating sweets .
56. Here's some free software. Why don't you .... it .... ?
57. You are exhausted. You feel like you will ....
58. She believes whatever you tell her. It's easy to .... her ..... .
59. You are feeling discouraged. You want to ....
60. This invention is so useful! It will ....

46

UNIT 7

PHRASAL VERBS

look up to	cheer up	look down on	put (someone) off (2)
look forward to	put up with	soak up	break up (2)
tell off	beat up	go for	calm down

look up to - You look up to someone that you admire and respect.
e.g. Tim really looks up to his dad; he imitates everything he does!

cheer up - You cheer up when you begin to feel happier or more hopeful.
e.g. Cheer up! Failing an exam is not the end of the world.

put (someone) off (2) - Something puts you off when it makes you unwilling or unable to do what you had intended or wanted to do.
e.g. Oh, you've stopped eating! Sorry, did all my talk about worms put you off your food?

look down on - Someone who looks down on you thinks that you are not very important, or less important than they are.
e.g. Unfortunately, in many countries, economic immigrants are looked down on.

look forward to - You look forward to something that is going to happen when you feel happy because you know that you will enjoy it.
e.g. I'm starving; I've been looking forward to having lunch all morning!

put up with - You put up with something unpleasant when you accept it or tolerate it.
e.g. You don't have to put up with being yelled at every day for no reason; I would find a new job if I were you.

soak up - Something such as a sponge soaks up liquid when it absorbs it or takes it up into itself.
e.g. Use the mop to soak up the water on the floor after you have a shower.

break up (2) - You break something up when you stop it.
e.g. The police used tear gas to try to break up the riot.

tell off - You tell someone off when you speak angrily to them because they have done something wrong.
e.g. The neighbours will tell you off if you play your stereo really loudly.

beat up - Someone is beaten up when they are punched, hit or kicked violently and repeatedly.
e.g. In some places, if you wear expensive looking jewellery you may be beaten up and robbed.

go for - You go for someone when you attack them, either physically or with words.
e.g. Okay, so I made a mistake. You didn't need to go for me like that and tell everyone what I did and how foolish it was.

calm down - You calm down when you stop feeling anxious, upset or angry.
e.g. When you feel angry, sometimes going for a walk can help you calm down.

Illustrated Phrasal Verbs

A. Fill in the gaps in the sentences below with the correct Phrasal Verb from unit 7.

1. It's great that Johnny has a musician that he ..looks up to.. , but I think he needs to work on developing his own style.

4. Mr. Williams may have worked hard in his life, but it is still wrong for him to ..look down on.. less successful people.

2. Toby was felling sad when he came home from school, but he ..cheered up.. when his mother baked a cake.

5. Grandma always ..puts up with.. our endless questions with a smile.

3. John was ..put off.. his studying by the loud roadworks going on outside the window.

6. Beatrice is ..looking forward to.. going sailing on her summer holidays.

Unit 7

7. Ian got ...told off... by his teacher for spray-painting graffiti on the wall.

10. When my sister and I were young, mother always ...broke up... our fights.

8. It took Billy several hours to ...calm down... after the bully made him get off the swings.

11. Use a tea towel to ...soak up... the water on the dishes before you put them away.

9. As Joey was walking home, another boy ...beat him up... and stole his mobile phone.

12. I was walking in the desert on my own when this crazy man with a club ...went for me... for no reason at all!

49

Illustrated Phrasal Verbs

B. Choose the correct answer A, B, C or D.

13. .... ! Not winning the award is not such a big deal; you won't even remember it in twenty years.
    a. Soak up
    b. Cheer up
    c. Break up
    d. Put off

14. It is unusual for children to physically .... other children in school though teasing and bullying is common.
    a. cheer up
    b. beat up
    c. put off
    d. look down on

15. Although I admire this singer's work, I wouldn't say I .... her. Her life is a mess!
    a. look down on
    b. look up to
    c. look forward to
    d. put up with

16. Don't let Todd's shyness .... you .... ; once you get to know him you will see that he has an amazing sense of humour.
    a. put ... off
    b. calm ... down
    c. tell ... off
    d. break ... up

17. If you saw a fight happening would you try to .... it ..... or not?
    a. calm ... down
    b. break ... up
    c. beat ... up
    d. put ... off

18. That dog is scared; if you corner him, he may .... you.
    a. beat up
    b. put up with
    c. look forward to
    d. go for

19. How do you .... such noisy inconsiderate neighbours?
    a. look down on
    b. break up
    c. put up with
    d. calm down

20. Laura likes to take baths because they .... her .... after a stressful day.
    a. cheer ... up
    b. break ... up
    c. soak ... up
    d. calm ... down

21. If my brother said something racist I would .... him ....
    a. beat ... up
    b. calm ... down
    c. tell ... off
    d. put ... off

22. We really need some bread to .... the sauce left on our plates.
    a. beat up
    b. go for
    c. soak up
    d. break up

23. Do your parents .... retiring so that they can travel?
    a. look forward to
    b. put up with
    c. go for
    d. look down on

24. Some people .... others because of the kind of clothes they wear.
    a. look down on
    b. go for
    c. break up
    d. cheer up

50

Unit 7

C. Match the Definitions with the correct Phrasal Verb. There are 3 extra Phrasal Verbs that do not match with any Definition.

25. To admire and respect someone
26. To begin to feel happier
27. To stop someone from doing something they had planned or wanted to do because of something else
28. To think that someone is less important than you are
29. To wait happily for something that is going to happen
30. To tolerate something unpleasant
31. To absorb liquid
32. To stop something from happening
33. To speak angrily to someone who has done something wrong
34. To punch or kick someone repeatedly
35. To attack someone physically or with words
36. To stop feeling anxious, angry or upset

25.	c
26.	j
27.	g
28.	o
29.	a
30.	k
31.	b
32.	l
33.	m
34.	e
35.	n
36.	h

a. look forward to
b. soak up
c. look up to
d. cut down on
e. beat up
f. look round
g. put off
h. calm down
i. drop off
j. cheer up
k. put up with
l. break up
m. tell off
n. go for
o. look down on

D. Fill in the gaps with the correct Phrasal Verb.

Don't turn your nose up at me!

When I was twelve or thirteen I really (37) **looked up to** a singer in a band. When I was a few years older I got tickets to see this band, and I (38) **looked forward** to the concert for weeks. After the concert I waited to try to meet the band. They came out to speak to us but they were really rude. They acted like they could barely (39) **put up with** the fans' questions, and I felt like they (40) **looked down on** us because we liked them. I was really sad for a while, and nothing could (41) **cheer** me **up**. Actually, the experience (42) **put** me **off** their music.

Break it up!

I saw a man get (43) **beaten up** today. Some guy just (44) **went for** him for no reason at all and kept kicking and punching him. Some other people tried to (45) **break up** the fight, and managed to hold the attacker down. The man had a bloody nose, so I gave him some tissue to (46) **soak up** the blood, and I called the police. By the time the police arrived everyone had (47) **calmed down** somewhat. The police (48) **told off** the people who stopped the fight, because they had done something dangerous and could have been hurt.

Illustrated Phrasal Verbs

E. Do the crossword finding the correct Phrasal Verb from unit 7.

Across
49. You broke you mother's vase. She will .... you ....
50. Your children are having a fight. You will .... it ....
51. It's your birthday next week. You .... it.
52. That bully doesn't like you. He might .... you ....
53. You are afraid of cats. You think they might .... you at any moment.
54. You are trying to study and your brother is playing video games. The noise will .... you ....

Down
55. You admire your mother and want to be like her. You .... her .
56. You spilled your coffee. Get a sponge to .... it ....
57. Your friend is moody but you care about him so you .... his moods .
58. Your friend is sad. You tell a joke to .... her ....
59. You don't have much money. A rich person might .... you.
60. Your mother thought you were lost and she's upset. You tell her to ....

52

UNIT 8

PHRASAL VERBS

tear up	check in	make out (2)	take up
fill in	take down	take over	pass away/on/over
turn into	wear off	brush up	die out

tear up - You tear something up when you destroy it completely by ripping it into pieces.
e.g. *Did you tear up the letter because you were angry?*

check in - You check in when you arrive somewhere, and let the people involved know that you are there.
e.g. *You must check in two hours before your flight is scheduled to leave.*

make out (2) - You make out things like checks or receipts when you write the necessary details on them.
e.g. *It's been so long since I've used one that I've forgotten how to make out a check!*

take up - You take something up when you start doing it as a regular activity, hobby or job.
e.g. *If you are bored, then you should take up a hobby.*

fill in - You fill something in when you write information in the spaces required.
e.g. *Getting a bank account always involves filling in a form.*

take down - You take something down when you make a written note of it.
e.g. *Let me take down your phone number just in case Ms. Witsthorpe doesn't have it.*

take over - You take over when you gain control of or responsibility for something in place of someone else.
e.g. *Will you take over steering the boat while I go and get a glass of water?*

pass away/pass on - You say that someone has passed away or passed on when they have died.
e.g. *Gina is sad because her grandfather passed away last week.*

turn into - The act of changing and becoming something or someone different, or making something or someone do this.
e.g. *I think I will turn into a very distrustful person if I get robbed again.*

wear off - a feeling, or the effect of a drug, wears off when it becomes less and less noticeable and finally disappears.
e.g. *Hopefully her headache will be gone by the time the aspirin wears off.*

brush up on - You brush up on something when you refresh or improve your knowledge of it.
e.g. *You'd better brush up on your computer skills if you want to get a good job.*

die out - Living things die out when the whole group or kind dies.
e.g. *Many plants and animals will die out in the next ten years.*

Illustrated Phrasal Verbs

A. Fill in the gaps in the sentences below with the correct Phrasal Verb from unit 8.

1. Stacy **tore up** the notes that her friend gave her, so that the teacher couldn't read them to the class.

4. James **made out** the check for 10,000 Euros and bought the ring the first time he saw it.

2. You are only **checking in** to the hospital for three days! Why have you brought so much luggage?

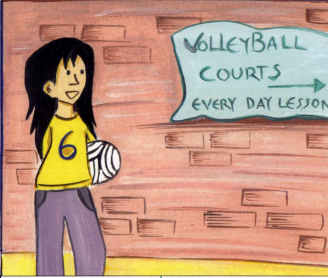

5. Holly was glad she had **taken up** volleyball, because it was now her favourite pastime.

3. **Filling in** job application forms is never easy.

6. The policeman who wrote him a parking ticket **took down** his name and driving license number.

Unit 8

7. Trish kissed the frog, and to her surprise it actually ..turned into.. a prince.

10. Even if the effects of your painkillers have ..worn off.. it's not a good idea to drink alcohol to get rid of your toothache!

8. Marko ..passed away.. in 1895 and was buried in this graveyard.

11. Because Trent took time to ..brush up on.. his English before travelling, he could easily communicate wherever he went.

9. When Mr. Smith retired, a new accountant ..took over.. his job.

12. The dinosaurs all ..died out.. a very long time ago.

55

Illustrated Phrasal Verbs

B. Choose the correct answer **A, B, C** or **D**.

13. You can pay by credit card when you .... to the hotel.
    a. turn in
    b. fill in
    c. brush up on
    d. check in

14. The giant pandas may .... if action is not taken to save their habitat.
    a. tear up
    b. take out
    c. die out
    d. fill in

15. Did you see that horror movie where the man .... a wolf?
    a. turns into
    b. takes up
    c. takes down
    d. takes over

16. Hosting an exchange student is a good opportunity to .... a foreign language you used to study.
    a. fill in
    b. take up
    c. make up
    d. brush up on

17. She asked if I could .... a receipt because she needed it for tax purposes.
    a. fill in
    b. make out
    c. take down
    d. tear up

18. My father used to be a hunter, but then he decided to .... bird watching instead.
    a. brush up on
    b. take up
    c. turn into
    d. take over

19. Don't .... that magazine! I want to keep it.
    a. die out
    b. fill in
    c. tear up
    d. wear off

20. I hope to .... my father's business one day when I am older.
    a. take over
    b. wear off
    c. fill in
    d. turn into

21. How long will it take for the excitement of living in a new place to .... ?
    a. pass away
    b. take over
    c. die out
    d. wear off

22. Just let me .... your details and we will try to solve the problem and get back to you.
    a. check in
    b. take up
    c. make out
    d. take down

23. At least Mr. Boyle .... peacefully in his sleep.
    a. took over
    b. passed away
    c. died out
    d. wore off

24. Did you .... all your application forms for university?
    a. take down
    b. fill in
    c. make out
    d. take up

Unit 8

Match the Definitions with the correct Phrasal Verb. There are 3 extra Phrasal Verbs that do not match with any Definition.

25. To destroy something by ripping it into pieces
26. To let people know that you have arrived somewhere
27. To write the necessary details on something such as a cheque
28. To begin doing something regularly such as a hobby
29. To write information in the spaces required
30. To make a written note of something.
31. To gain responsibility for something in the place of someone else
32. When someone dies
33. To cause something to become something else
34. When an effect becomes less and less noticeable and finally disappears
35. To improve or refresh your knowledge of something
36. When a whole group of one kind of creature dies

25.	c
26.	h
27.	k
28.	b
29.	n
30.	e
31.	g
32.	d
33.	m
34.	i
35.	o
36.	f

a. work out
b. take up
c. tear up
d. pass away
e. take down
f. die out
g. take over
h. check in
i. wear off
j. point out
k. make out
l. put on
m. turn into
n. fill in
o. brush up (on)

Fill in the gaps with the correct Phrasal Verb.

Taking up a new hobby

One day Jill decided that she wanted to (37) **take up** glass blowing. She (38) **filled out** all the appropriate forms and enrolled in a class. On the first day, she (39) **checked in** at the college registrar's office and they (40) **took down** some information like her mailing address and an emergency contact number. She also (41) **made out** a cheque to pay for the course, but was embarrassed because she put her name in the wrong place and had to (42) **tear up** the check and write another one. As the semester went on, she enjoyed the class a lot, but unfortunately the instructor quit when his mother (43) **passed away** and a new instructor (44) **took over**. The class then (45) **turned into** something completely different! The instructor didn't know much about blowing glass, but she talked endlessly about all the species of animals that were (46) **dying out** because of the actions of humans. Her enthusiasm for the subject never seemed to (47) **wear off** and she insisted that her students all (48) **brush up on** their knowledge of environmental issues even though we were there to learn to blow glass.

Illustrated Phrasal Verbs

E. Do the crossword finding the correct Phrasal Verb from unit 8.

Across
49. Take these pills every four hours. Otherwise the effects will ....
50. You don't have cash with you. You will .... a check.
51. You've forgotten how to speak Spanish. You need to .... on it.
52. You must remember what was said at the meeting. You should .... some notes.
53. Gorillas are endangered. They might ....
54. You want a library card. You will have to .... a form .
55. Your boss is on holiday for a week. You will .... while he is gone.
56. Puppies can be naughty. They often .... things ....

Down
57. That boy was bitten by a bat. Will he .... a vampire?
58. You just arrived at the hotel. You need to ....
59. You want to meet people. You should .... a team sport.
60. No one lives forever. Everyone will .... eventually.

UNIT 9

PHRASAL VERBS

get away with	let down	get away	own up
let out	let off	turn down	drop out
carry out	fall through	lay off	put forward

get away with - You get away with something illegal or dishonest when you manage to avoid being caught or punished for it.
e.g. I doubt that you will get away with telling people you're a lawyer. What if they ask you a question?

let down - You let someone down if you do not do what you promised to do or what he or she expected you to do.
e.g. My friends really let me down when none of them came to my birthday party.

get away - You get away when you escape.
e.g. The little boy was struggling to get away from his mother and run after the ice-cream lorry.

own up - You own up when you admit you were the one who did something that was wrong.
e.g. No one in the office would own up to breaking the computer.

let out - You let someone out when you allow them to leave, usually by opening or unlocking a door.
e.g. This neighbourhood gets very noisy around 3pm when the children are let out of school.

let off - Someone is let off when he or she is given a punishment that is less severe than deserved, or no punishment at all.
e.g. I will let you off this time but don't do it again!

turn down - You turn someone or something down when you refuse what they are offering or asking.
e.g. That cake looks delicious but since I'm on a diet I will have to turn it down.

drop out - You drop out of an activity when you take no further part in it.
e.g. If you drop out of school you will have a hard time finding a job.

carry out - You carry out a task or procedure when you do it, complete it, or put it into practice.
e.g. That's a fantastic idea, but do you think you can actually carry it out?

fall through - A plan falls through when it fails or cannot be achieved.
e.g. Our plan to go on a picnic this weekend will fall through if it rains.

lay off - A company lays people off when it stops employing them either permanently or temporarily.
e.g. If the economy does poorly businesses will be forced to lay off hundreds of people.

put forward - You put forward an idea when you suggest it for other people's consideration.
e.g. The solution that Tina put forward was so simple that everyone was amazed they hadn't thought of it themselves.

Illustrated Phrasal Verbs

A. Fill in the gaps in the sentences below with the correct Phrasal Verb from unit 9.

1. Maurice ..got away with.. robbing the bank and is now enjoying life on a tropical island

4. How on earth did the patient manage to ..get away.. from the security guards and escape?

2. Jane finally ..owned up.. to breaking the vase.

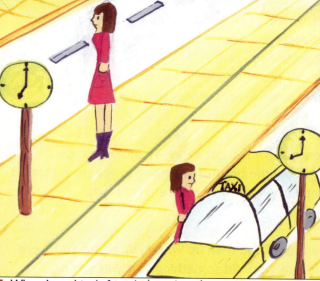

5. When Josephine's friends ..let.. her ..down.. by forgetting to give her a ride home, she called a taxi.

3. Who ..let.. the elephant ..out.. of his cage?

6. The judge ..let.. him ..off.. with a very light punishment even though the jury thought that he was guilty.

Unit 9

7. His ambition to be on the football team ..fell through.. when he was hit by a car.

10. Jimmy finally decided to ..drop out.. of school when he realized he was just not interested in studying!

8. Mr. Fredreckson could not believe that he was ..turned down.. by yet another employer.

11. That crate is heavy; do you think that Louise can actually ..carry out.. the task you asked her to do?

9. When the clothing factory closed down, many people were ..laid off.. .

12. Today the teacher ..put forward.. the idea of going on a hike, and the whole class agreed.

Illustrated Phrasal Verbs

B. Choose the correct answer **A**, **B**, **C** or **D**.

13. Although he was speeding, the police man .... him .... with only a small fine.
    a. put ... forward
    b. let ... down
    c. let ... off
    d. let ... out

14. Bob was truly a different person after he .... prison.
    a. was let out of
    b. was let off to
    c. got away with
    d. got away in

15. Can anyone .... some kind of solution for this problem?
    a. fall through
    b. put forward
    c. get away with
    d. turn down

16. It is rare for someone to .... fraud for more than a few years without being found out.
    a. own up
    b. get away
    c. let out
    d. get away with

17. If I were you I'd .... to making the mistake; it's the responsible thing to do.
    a. fall through
    b. own up
    c. put forward
    d. carry out

18. When the famous painting went missing the police decided to .... an investigation.
    a. put forward
    b. own up
    c. let down
    d. carry out

19. Why would anyone ever want to .... of school and start working when they are so young?
    a. turn down
    b. carry out
    c. drop out
    d. get away

20. She felt terribly .... when she found out that her best friend had told her secret to everybody.
    a. let off
    b. let out
    c. put forward
    d. let down

21. Although he didn't really want to go skiing, he didn't want to .... their invitation in case he offended them.
    a. turn down
    b. carry out
    c. fall through
    d. drop out

22. If they .... him .... he will take the opportunity to go back to school and get a Master's degree.
    a. drop ... out
    b. get ... away
    c. lay ... off
    d. put ... forward

23. Do you know how to .... if an attacker grabs your arm?
    a. drop out
    b. turn down
    c. let off
    d. get away

24. Do you have an alternative in mind in case your plans for the weekend .... ?
    a. fall through
    b. carry out
    c. let down
    d. lay off

62

Unit 9

C. Match the Definitions with the correct Phrasal Verb. There are 3 extra Phrasal Verbs that do not match with any Definition.

25. To avoid being caught or punished for doing something illegal or dishonest
26. To fail to do something you promised someone you would do
27. To escape
28. To admit that you were the one who did something wrong
29. To allow someone to leave by opening or unlocking a door
30. To be given a punishment less severe than what you deserved
31. To refuse what someone is asking or offering
32. To no longer take part in something
33. To do, complete, or put something into practice
34. When something can no longer possibly happen
35. To stop employing someone
36. To suggest something for the consideration of others

25.	i
26.	k
27.	f
28.	h
29.	a
30.	e
31.	j
32.	o
33.	c
34.	d
35.	m
36.	l

a. let out
b. turn down
c. carry out
d. fall through
e. let off
f. get away
g. put through
h. own up
i. get away with
j. turn down
k. let down
l. put forward
m. lay off
n. take out
o. drop out

D. Fill in the gaps with the correct Phrasal Verb.

There's no escape!

If you think you will (37) **get away with** stealing my money, you are wrong. It will be better for you to (38) **own up** and admit that you made a mistake because then you probably will be (39) **let off** with an lighter punishment when we go to court, and maybe all the people that you (40) **let down** will even be able to forgive you. It is no good trying to (41) **get away**. If you try to leave the country I guarantee you that you won't be able to (42) **carry out** your plan. You are going to jail, and you won't be (43) **let out** for a long, long time.

Let's get down to business!

Joshua decided to (44) **drop out** of school because he had a fantastic business idea that would make him rich before he was twenty. He thought he would borrow a few thousand from his parents to get started, and then there would be no looking back. However his plan (45) **fell through** when his father was (46) **laid off**, and when his request for a loan was (47) **turned down**. Joshua was very disappointed, but then he had an idea! If he could get his father excited about his business venture, they could go into a partnership and start the business together! After all, his father needed something to do now. Cautiously, he (48) **put** the idea **forward** to his father. It was a bit risky, and he wasn't sure his father would be willing to take the chance. His father insisted on a few changes to the business plan, but then, to Joshua's surprise, agreed.

Illustrated Phrasal Verbs

E. Do the crossword finding the correct Phrasal Verb from unit 9.

			(55)				(57)				(59)		(60)
			d				p		(58)		l		l
			r				u		f		e		e
			o	(49)	g	e	t	a	w	a	y		t
			p				f		l		d		o
			o	(56)			o		(50)	l	a	y	o	f	f
			u	c			r			t		w		f
(51)	g	e	t	a	w	a	y	w	i	t	h		n		
	(54)			r			a			r			
	l			r	(52)	t	u	r	n	d	o	w	n
	e			y			d			u			
	t			o						g			
(53)	o	w	n	u	p					h			
	u			t									
	t												

Across

49. We've caught you now! You can't ....
50. Your business is not making money. You must ...... someone ....
51. You got caught shoplifting. You can't .... it .
52. You don't want to go to the movies with him. You will .... him ....
53. You feel bad about what you did. You will .... and apologize.

Down

54. The dog is barking at the door. Please .... him ....
55. You are feeling very homesick at college. You may ....
56. You have been given instructions. You must now .... them ....
57. Your friend has a problem. You .... a solution.
58. You should keep several options in mind. Your plans might ....
59. Your friend did not do what he promised. You feel ....
60. You didn't get punished. You were ....

UNIT 10

PHRASAL VERBS

go off	put out	blow up (1)	cut down on
blow up (2)	break off	get through (2)	hold up (2)
run out of	break into	burn down	wear out

go off - A bomb or gun goes off when it explodes or is fired.
e.g. Don't point a gun at anyone you don't intend to shoot. You never know, it might go off.

put out - You put out a fire when you extinguish it.
e.g. I panicked when the toaster caught on fire, but my housemate threw a towel over the fire and put it out.

blow up (1) - You blow something up when you destroy it with a bomb or other exploding weapon.
e.g. These days everyone is worried that terrorists will try to blow up an airplane.

cut down on - You cut down on something when you do or use it less than you did before.
e.g. Don't offer Betty that cake; she's trying very hard to cut down on the amount of sugar she eats.

blow up (2) - You blow up something such as a tyre or a balloon when you fill it with air.
e.g. I hope you have a pump to blow up that air mattress, otherwise it is going to take forever.

break out - Violent or disturbing situations break out when they begin, often suddenly.
e.g. I was sound asleep until the fight broke out in the street below my window.

get through (2) - You get through work or a task when you finish or complete it.
e.g. Do you think you'll be able to get through reading the report before the meeting?

hold up (2) - You hold up people or things when you use a gun to rob them.
e.g. Did you receive training about what to do if someone tries to hold up your shop?

run out of - You run out of something when there is no more of it left.
e.g. If you had told me we'd run out of milk, I would have bought more on the way home.

break into - Someone breaks into a building when he or she enters by force, usually with the intention of stealing or doing mischief.
e.g. Someone broke into the government building and stole important papers.

burn down - A building burns down when it is destroyed by fire.
e.g. The protesters attempted to burn down the bank.

wear out - You wear out someone when you tire them greatly, exhaust them.
e.g. You will wear your brother out if you make him go running with you in the morning, and then shopping in the afternoon!

Illustrated Phrasal Verbs

A. Fill in the gaps in the sentences below with the correct Phrasal Verb from unit 10.

1. When the bomb ..went off.. it made an awful, loud noise.

4. My little brother loves to ..blow up.. balloons.

2. Many forest fires ..broke out.. last summer and a great many trees were destroyed.

5. Billy did ..put out.. his cigarette when the security guard told him to, but as soon as the guard left he lit it again.

3. Though Timothy has ..cut down on.. his drinking, it would be better if he gave up alcohol all together.

6. Did you see who threw the grenade that ..blew up.. the building?

Unit 10

7. The robber ..broke into.. the bank by throwing a brick through the window.

10. Billy ..got through.. a whole novel this weekend for his English class.

8. Layla got up in the middle of the night to make a sandwich, but found that she had ..run out of.. of everything, even bread!

11. Lisa was working as a teller when the bank was ..held up.. .

9. Did you see the flames when the warehouse across the road ..burned down..?

12. Look at Tony! He must be completely ..worn out.. from loading all those kegs onto the lorry.

67

Illustrated Phrasal Verbs

B. Choose the correct answer **A**, **B**, **C** or **D**.

13. In South Africa, robbers sometimes .... drivers when they are stopped at stoplights.
    a. blow up
    b. break into
    c. wear out
    d. hold up

14. You can easily be injured if fireworks .... in your hands before you throw them.
    a. go off
    b. burn down
    c. blow up
    d. break out

15. It is bad news for everyone when wars ....
    a. break out
    b. get through
    c. blow up
    d. go off

16. We'd better fill up the car before we .... petrol.
    a. get through
    b. wear out
    c. cut down on
    d. run out of

17. They lost all their old photographs when their house .... in the fire of 1992.
    a. went off
    b. blew up
    c. held up
    d. burned down

18. The workers are going to .... the building in order to demolish it.
    a. put out
    b. go off
    c. wear out
    d. blow up

19. How many balloons do we need to .... for the party?
    a. put out
    b. blow up
    c. break out
    d. hold up

20. People say walking a dog is good exercise, but my dog always seems to ....me............ in next to no time.
    a. break out
    b. wear out
    c. run out of
    d. get through

21. Could you please .... the lights? I'm trying to sleep.
    a. blow up
    b. put out
    c. cut down on
    d. hold up

22. I have a huge list of e-mails to .... this morning.
    a. run out of
    b. get through
    c. cut down on
    d. go off

23. I had to .... my own apartment last night because I locked myself out.
    a. blow up
    b. go off
    c. break into
    d. hold up

24. Tara has .... smoking, but she hasn't quit.
    a. run out of
    b. cut down on
    c. put out
    d. broken into

Unit 10

C. Match the Definitions with the correct Phrasal Verb. There are 3 extra Phrasal Verbs that do not match with any Definition.

25. When a bomb explodes or a gun is fired
26. To extinguish something
27. To destroy something with a bomb
28. To do or use something less than you did before
29. To fill something with air
30. When a violent or disturbing situation begins suddenly
31. To complete a task
32. To use a gun to rob someone
33. When there is no more left of something
34. To enter a building by force
35. To destroy something with fire
36. To exhaust someone.

25.	d
26.	a
27.	g or n
28.	l
29.	n or g
30.	i
31.	e
32.	f
33.	k
34.	h
35.	o
36.	m

a. put out
b. find out
c. do up
d. go off
e. get through
f. hold up
g. blow up
h. break into
i. break out
j. put on
k. run out of
l. cut down on
m. wear out
n. blow up
o. burn down

D. Fill in the gaps with the correct Phrasal Verb.

It could happen to you, but it probably won't!

Often we tend to believe that bad things won't happen to us. The bank that is set on fire and (37) ..burned down.. by anarchists won't be my branch and the flight that is (38) ..blown up.. by terrorists will not be the one that I or anyone close to me is on. That nuclear reactor down the road will not overheat and (39) ..go off.. . I don't (40) ..carry out.. regular maintenance on my car, yet that person who was injured when his brakes failed couldn't have been me. We don't expect to be (41) ..held up.. at gunpoint on the street or to have our houses (42) ..broken into.. every time we go out. We don't feel that we need to (43) ..cut down on.. cigarettes and alcohol because, hey, we are young and healthy. We neither expect that a war will (44) ..break out.. in our neighbourhoods or that the supermarkets will (45) ..run out of.. milk. Is this foolish? After all, these things do happen and what is more, people sometimes collapse and die while (46) ..blowing up.. balloons or watching TV. Perhaps our lack of concern is foolish, particularly, if it is something we could do something about. Your toaster may catch on fire one day, so know how to (47) ..put.. it ..out.. when it does. But perhaps for things we can't control, it is a protection mechanism we should be grateful for. Imagine how life would (48) ..wear.. us ..out.. if we worried that some terrible disaster was going to happen at every step we took!

69

Illustrated Phrasal Verbs

E. Do the crossword finding the correct Phrasal Verb from unit 10.

				(56)		(57)								
		(55)		g		g								
		c		o		e								(60)
(49)	r	u	n	o	u	t	o	f	(59)					b
		t		f		t			b					l
		d		f		h		(50)| b	r	e	a	k	i	n	t	o
		o				r			e					w
	(51)	w	e	a	r	o	u	t	a					u
		n				u		(58)	k					p
		o				g		b	o					
		n		(52)	h	o	l	d	u	p				
								o		t				
	(53)	b	u	r	n	d	o	w	n					
								u						
					(54)	p	u	t	o	u	t			

Unit 10

Across

49. You have no sugar in the house. You have .... it.
50. You are afraid someone might .... your house. You buy a burglar alarm.
51. You are working too hard. It will .... you ....
52. You called the police. Someone tried to .... your shop.
53. You forgot to turn off the stove before you left. Your house could ....
54. A small fire starts while you are cooking. You must .... it ....

Down

55. You want to lose weight. You need to .... fatty foods.
56. You cover your ears. You don't like it when firecrackers ....
57. You have a lot of homework to do. You are afraid you won't .... it all.
58. Your tires are getting a little flat. You need to .... them .... again.
59. There is a lot of tension at the borders of your country. A war might ....
60. You are afraid to fly. The plane might ....

Illustrated Phrasal Verbs

Review Units 6-10

Revision Test 2: Units 6-10

A. Match the first half of the sentence with the second half containing the correct Phrasal Verb.

1. I haven't spoken French for nearly five years so I need to
2. We are evacuating the building because we think a bomb might
3. If cats or dogs are fighting it is dangerous to try to
4. I'm going to have to go to the corner shop; I think we've
5. When the neighbours' son threw a ball through my window, I had to
6. After only a few minutes of fighting, the smaller child had to
7. He didn't like statistics at all and decided to
8. I haven't smoked for years; I was forced to
9. The murderer felt guilty and scared and decided to
10. I'm tired from preparing for the party; I can't
11. There are lots of firemen near the new shopping centre because of a threat that it may
12. You got caught stealing? It's amazing you were
13. The masked man pulled out a gun and proceeded to
14. Don't waste energy; when you leave the house you should
15. He stopped smoking last year, but now he needs to
16. Even the best thought out plans can
17. After we arrive, we will go directly to
18. His music teacher was the only person that Tom used to
19. Smell the milk before you put it in your coffee; it may
20. When will the next president

1.	l
2.	p
3.	c
4.	d
5.	q
6.	s
7.	i
8.	o
9.	f
10.	j
11.	n
12.	r
13.	a
14.	h
15.	m
16.	t
17.	b
18.	e
19.	g
20.	k

a. hold up the bank.
b. check in at the hotel.
c. break them up.
d. run out of chocolate.
e. look up to.
f. give himself up.
g. have gone off.
h. put out the lights.
i. drop out of the class.
j. blow up another balloon!
k. take over the Whitehouse?
l. brush up on it.
m. cut down on sugar, too.
n. burn down.
o. give up ages ago!
p. go off.
q. tell him off.
r. let off so easily!
s. give in and stop.
t. fall through.

73

Illustrated Phrasal Verbs

B. Write C or I in the box to the left (Correct or Incorrect) for each sentence using a Phrasal Verb.

21.	A few pandas have died out.	21.	I
22.	She will get round her dad; he will buy her the toy eventually.	22.	C
23.	He felt beaten up when his girlfriend yelled at him in public.	23.	I
24.	Can I take down a cheque? I don't have any cash on me at the moment.	24.	I
25.	Someone broke into my aunty's house and stole all her jewellery.	25.	C
26.	The car accelerated and passed away around the corner.	26.	I
27.	When her husband left her, she tore up all their old letters.	27.	C
28.	You had better take up cleaning your room when I tell you!	28.	I
29.	It makes me feel sad when you are sad, so please cheer up.	29.	C
30.	You shouldn't give up a task just because it is difficult.	30.	C
31.	I am taller than my little brother so I have to look down on him.	31.	I
32.	When the alcohol wears off, I think she will have a hangover.	32.	C
33.	I hope they never let that vile murderer out of jail!	33.	C
34.	The fire blew up suddenly because it was very hot and dry.	34.	I
35.	His mood turned down when he read the newspaper because there was so much bad news.	35.	I
36.	She put off her jacket because it was warm inside the building.	36.	I
37.	This is fire country; several houses burn down every summer.	37.	C
38.	Boys often look up to famous sports figures.	38.	C
39.	It is extremely rude for guests to go through their hosts' cupboards!	39.	C
40.	That bug is so perfectly camouflaged, that it is easy to mistake it for a stick.	40.	C

Revision Test 2: Units 6-10

C. Fill in the gaps in the text with the correct tense of the Phrasal Verbs from the box below.

- take in - drop off - own up - put forward
- soak up - break out - wear out - get through
- let down - get away with - fill in - look forward to
- go for - carry out - try out - wear out - run out of
- turn into - put up with - lay off - calm down

The pressure takes its toll...

Last Friday at the office there was a huge amount of work to (41) get through. We were all already (42) worn out from the difficult week and Natalie was actually (43) dropping off over her keyboard. I suppose everyone blamed me because I had (44) put forward the idea to do the proposal. I will (45) own up that I was a bit (46) taken in by the glamour of opening a branch somewhere in the tropics. It would still be work, but it would also be a chance to (47) try out something new and maybe even (48) soak up some sun! But today we had dozens of forms to (49) fill in and tasks to (50) carry out, and we were (51) running out of time because the deadline was approaching fast!

I guess it was inevitable that some sort of dispute would (52) break out because of the pressure we were under, but I was still shocked when Nancy decided, completely out of the blue, to (53) go for Natalie. "What's this? Sleeping? Why do those of us who are trying to work have to (54) put up with the others who (55) let us down by trying to (56) get away with doing nothing all day? You should be (57) laid off for your laziness! "(58) Calm down, Nancy!" I said. "You don't need to (59) turn a little nap into such a big deal!" I was (60) looking forward to the weekend, that is for sure!

75

Phrasal Verbs Index

is off: unit 5
go off: unit 6

be over: unit 5

be taken aback: unit 5

beat up: unit 7

blow up (1): unit 10
blow up (2): unit 10

break down (1): unit 2
break down (2): unit 3
break into: unit 10
break off: unit 10
break off: unit 2
break out in: unit 3
break up (1): unit 2
break up (2): unit 7

bring up: unit 1

brush up on: unit 8

burn down: unit 10

call off: unit 5

calm down: unit 7

carry out: unit 9

catch on: unit 6

check in: unit 8

cheer up: unit 7

come across: unit 3
come into: unit 3
come round/come to: unit 3
come up with: unit 4

cut down on: unit 10
cut off: unit 2

die out: unit 8

do up (2): unit 5
do up: unit 1

drop in: unit 3
drop off (1): unit 4
drop off: unit 6
drop out: unit 9

fall out: unit 2
fall through: unit 9

fill in: unit 8

find out- unit 1

get away with: unit 9
get away: unit 9
get over: unit 3
get round (1): unit 3
get round: unit 6
get through (1): unit 2
get through (2): unit 10

give (oneself) up (1): unit 6
give in: unit 6
give out: unit 5
give up (2): unit 6
give up (3): unit 6

go down: unit 3
go for: unit 7
go off: unit 10
go through: unit 6
go with: unit 5

grow up: unit 1

hold on: unit 2
hold up (1): unit 4
hold up (2): unit 10

lay off: unit 9

let down: unit 9
let off: unit 9
let out: unit 9

look after: unit 1
look back on: unit 1
look down on: unit 7
look for: unit 1
look forward to: unit 7
look into: unit 1
look over: unit 1
look round: unit 1
look up to: unit 7
look up: unit 1

make out (1): unit 4

make out (2): unit 8

make up (1): unit 2

make up (2): unit 4

make up for: unit 2

mistake for: unit 6

own up: unit 9

pass away/on: unit 8

pass out: unit 3

pick up: unit 4

point out: unit 4

put (someone) off (2): unit 7

put forward: unit 9

put off (1): unit 5

put on: unit 5

put out: unit 10

put through: unit 2

put up with: unit 7

run in: unit 3

run into: unit 3

run out of: unit 10

see off: unit 4

set off: unit 4

soak up: unit 7

speak up: unit 2

stand for: unit 2

take after: unit 1

take down: unit 8

take in: unit 6

take off (1): unit 4

take off (2): unit 5

take over

take up: unit 8

tear up: unit 8

tell off: unit 7

think over: unit 4

try on: unit 5

try out: unit 6

turn down: unit 9

turn into: unit 8

wear off: unit 8

wear out (1): unit 5

wear out: unit 10

work out: unit 4

Irregular Verbs Index

Base Form	Simple Past Tense	Past Participle
awake	awoke	awoken
be	was, were	been
bear	bore	born
beat	beat	beaten
become	became	become
begin	began	begun
bend	bent	bent
beset	beset	beset
bet	bet	bet
bid	bid/bade	bid/bidden
bind	bound	bound
bite	bit	bitten
bleed	bled	bled
blow	blew	blown
break	broke	broken
breed	bred	bred
bring	brought	brought
broadcast	broadcast	broadcast
build	built	built
burn	burned/burnt	burned/burnt
burst	burst	burst
buy	bought	bought
cast	cast	cast
catch	caught	caught
choose	chose	chosen
cling	clung	clung
come	came	come
cost	cost	cost
creep	crept	crept
cut	cut	cut
deal	dealt	dealt
dig	dug	dug
dive	dived/dove	dived
do	did	done
draw	drew	drawn
dream	dreamed/dreamt	dreamed/dreamt
drive	drove	driven
drink	drank	drunk
eat	ate	eaten
fall	fell	fallen
feed	fed	fed
feel	felt	felt
fight	fought	fought
find	found	found
fit	fit	fit
flee	fled	fled
fling	flung	flung
fly	flew	flown
forbid	forbade	forbidden
forget	forgot	forgotten
forego (forgo)	forewent	foregone
forgive	forgave	forgiven
forsake	forsook	forsaken
freeze	froze	frozen
get	got	got/gotten
give	gave	given
go	went	gone
grind	ground	ground
grow	grew	grown
hang	hung	hung
hear	heard	heard
hide	hid	hidden
hit	hit	hit
hold	held	held
hurt	hurt	hurt
keep	kept	kept
kneel	knelt	knelt
knit	knit	knit
know	knew	known
lay	laid	laid
lead	led	led
leap	leaped/leapt	leaped/leapt

Base Form	Simple Past Tense	Past Participle
learn	learned/learnt	learned/learnt
leave	left	left
lend	lent	lent
let	let	let
lie	lay	lain
light	lighted/lit	lighted/lit
lose	lost	lost
make	made	made
mean	meant	meant
meet	met	met
misspell	misspelled/misspelt	misspelled/misspelt
mistake	mistook	mistaken
mow	mowed	mowed/mown
overcome	overcame	overcome
overdo	overdid	overdone
overtake	overtook	overtaken
overthrow	overthrew	overthrown
pay	paid	paid
plead	pled	pled
prove	proved	proved/proven
put	put	put
quit	quit	quit
read	read	read
rid	rid	rid
ride	rode	ridden
ring	rang	rung
rise	rose	risen
run	ran	run
saw	sawed	sawed/sawn
say	said	said
see	saw	seen
seek	sought	sought
sell	sold	sold
send	sent	sent
set	set	set
sew	sewed	sewed/sewn
shake	shook	shaken
shave	shaved	shaved/shaven
shear	shore	shorn
shed	shed	shed
shine	shone	shone
shoe	shoed	shoed/shod
shoot	shot	shot
show	showed	showed/shown
shrink	shrank	shrunk
shut	shut	shut
sing	sang	sung
sink	sank	sunk
sit	sat	sat
sleep	slept	slept
slay	slew	slain
slide	slid	slid
sling	slung	slung
slit	slit	slit
smite	smote	smitten
sow	sowed	sowed/sown
speak	spoke	spoken
speed	sped	sped
spend	spent	spent
spill	spilled/spilt	spilled/spilt
spin	spun	spun
spit	spit/spat	spit
split	split	split
spread	spread	spread
spring	sprang/sprung	sprung
stand	stood	stood
steal	stole	stolen
stick	stuck	stuck
sting	stung	stung

Irregular Verbs

Base Form	Simple Past Tense	Past Participle
stink	stank	stunk
stride	strode	stridden
strike	struck	struck
string	strung	strung
strive	strove	striven
swear	swore	sworn
sweep	swept	swept
swell	swelled	swelled/swollen
swim	swam	swum
swing	swung	swung
take	took	taken
teach	taught	taught
tear	tore	torn
tell	told	told
think	thought	thought
thrive	thrived/throve	thrived
throw	threw	thrown
thrust	thrust	thrust
tread	trod	trodden
understand	understood	understood
uphold	upheld	upheld
upset	upset	upset
wake	woke	woken
wear	wore	worn
weave	weaved/wove	weaved/woven
wed	wed	wed
weep	wept	wept
wind	wound	wound
win	won	won
withhold	withheld	withheld
withstand	withstood	withstood
wring	wrung	wrung
write	wrote	written